TIMELINES

1900s

by
Gail B. Stewart

CRESTWOOD HOUSE

New York

Library of Congress Cataloging In Publication Data
Stewart, Gail, 1949-
    1900s / by Gail B. Stewart.
    p. cm. — (Timelines)
    Includes index.
    Summary: History, trivia, and fun through photographs and articles present life
in the United States between 1900 and 1909.
    ISBN 0-89686-471-5
    1. History, Modern—20th century—Miscellanea—Juvenile literature. [1. United
States—History—1901-1909—Miscellanea.] I. Title. II. Series.
D422.S77   1989   973.91'1   89-9936

Photo credits
Cover: The Bettmann Archive: The assassination of President William McKinley
The Bettmann Archive: 4, 10, 11, 29, 30, 31, 32, 35, 38, 45, 46
Wide World Photos: 6, 7, 9, 13, 15, 16, 19, 23, 25, 26, 36, 43
FPG International: 20, 21, 40
Ford Motor Company: 39

On the front cover: The assassination of William
McKinley made headlines in 1901.

CRESTWOOD HOUSE

Macmillan Publishing Company
866 Third Avenue
New York, NY 10022
Collier Macmillan Canada, Inc.

Produced by Carnival Enterprises

Printed in the United States of America

First Edition

10 9 8 7 6 5 4 3 2

CONTENTS

INTRODUCTION

If you had been living in America in 1900, chances are you would have lived on a farm or in a small town. Most likely you wouldn't have owned a telephone. Only 2 percent of Americans did. There were no radios and no televisions. If you were one of the first in your town to own a car, you didn't have many places to drive it. There were only 150 miles of paved road in the entire country!

Historians sometimes refer to the decade of 1900–1909 as the "Age of Optimism." People were happy and excited to be part of a new century. Cars, telephones, and sewing machines were new inventions. It seemed as if every day someone was inventing something interesting. This made life just a little easier, a little more fun.

A young woman steers a gondola through a lagoon at the 1904 World's Fair.

HATCHET-ATION

In the year 1900, Carry Nation captured America's attention. She was part of the Women's Christian Temperance Union, an organization that tried to rid society of liquor (alcoholic beverages). The Union held prayer meetings and preached against the evils of drunkenness.

But six-foot-tall Carry Nation wasn't satisfied with speeches and prayer meetings. She felt it was her duty to make sure saloons and bars closed for good. Waving a razor-sharp hatchet (which later became her trademark), she would march into saloons. She smashed furniture, bottles, and anything else she could reach.

Carry Nation began her rampages in Kansas, but soon took her hatchet and her supporters into cities all around the country. "Hatchet-ation"—her term for the way she closed saloons—was not popular. She was arrested often for destruction of property. Sometimes she was spit upon and even shot at!

After one arrest, Carry Nation kneels in her jail cell.

Four years after the subway groundbreaking ceremonies, New York Mayor George McClellan and other city officials ride through the newly constructed subway.

She became famous, however, and her appearances in meeting halls earned her $300 a week. This, plus the money she made from selling souvenir hatchets, helped pay for all her court costs and fines.

BEGINNINGS OF NEW YORK'S SUBWAYS

New York had an official groundbreaking ceremony in 1900. The mayor dug the first shovelful of dirt for the city's new subway system. The first step was a $36 million tunnel under the East River. The tunnel would link Manhattan and Brooklyn.

By the close of the century, this system would become a spiderweb of 500 miles of subway track. Its aim then was the same as it is now—to help New Yorkers get around their huge city cheaply and quickly.

7

JOHANN'S AMAZING WALK

Johann Hurlinger set a world's record in 1900. He walked 871 miles, from Vienna to Paris—on his hands! He tried to set a pace of ten miles per day, every day, rain or shine. On some days he bettered his average. The trip took 55 days to complete.

SAY "CHEESE!"

The largest camera the world had ever seen was built in 1900. It was needed to take special pictures for the 1900 Paris Exposition. A railroad company wanted to display gigantic photographs of its new luxury train, the Alton Limited.

The camera was very successful. Called the Mammoth, the huge camera was 6 feet wide, 9 feet high, and 20 feet deep. The photographs it produced were about 5 feet by 8 feet! The Mammoth was not cheap to use. Fifteen people were needed to operate it. In addition, more than ten gallons of chemicals were needed to develop just one photograph!

AN OFFICIAL TERRITORY

In June, the Hawaiian Islands were officially made a territory of the United States. Becoming a territory is often the first step toward becoming a state. That didn't happen for Hawaii until 1959.

President McKinley strongly favored Hawaii's new status. He felt Hawaii was an important link between the United States, Japan, and China. He also felt Hawaii could be strategic in a military way.

Territories of the United States have governors just as states do. Hawaii's first governor was Sanford Dole, who had served as the president of Hawaii before the change.

MCKINLEY RE-ELECTED

On November 6, President William McKinley was re-elected to the White House. His running mate was Theodore Roosevelt, then governor of New York. McKinley gave his acceptance speech from the porch of his Ohio home. As usual, he wore a red carnation in his buttonhole.

In this election, McKinley and Roosevelt defeated Democrats William Jennings Bryan and Adlai Stevenson. The election wasn't even close. Americans were happy with the leadership that had brought them such prosperous times.

THE EMERALD CITY LOCATED

In 1900, L. Frank Baum wrote *The Wonderful Wizard of Oz* for his children and their playmates.

One of the children listening to the story had asked him the name of the Emerald City. But Baum hadn't given it any name at all. Not wanting to interrupt the children's storytime, he glanced around his office. He spotted his filing cabinets that were marked A–F, G–N, and O–Z. "Oz," he told the child. "The city's name was Oz!"

Jack Haley as the Tin Woodman, Judy Garland as Dorothy, and Ray Bolger as the Scarecrow starred in the 1939 movie version of L. Frank Baum's The Wonderful Wizard of Oz.

SPINDLETOP USHERS IN THE OIL BOOM

The little town of Beaumont, Texas, became a boom town when oil was discovered there on January 10. A well called Spindletop erupted and sent a fountain of oil more than 200 feet in the air.

Up until this time, almost all the oil in America was pumped from wells in the eastern part of the country. Experts said that Spindletop was producing as much oil as all the eastern wells put together!

The well's owners, Anthony Lucas and Patillo Higgins, weren't surprised. But the discovery of oil was a shock to almost everyone else. In fact, when Lucas had asked the Standard Oil Company for some financial backing, company officials laughed. Before the discovery, one Standard Oil executive was sure there was no oil west of the Mississippi River. He even offered to drink every gallon of oil Lucas could find!

Spindletop, the oil well that erupted in 1901

William McKinley and Theodore Roosevelt's campaign poster for the 1900 election

PRESIDENT ASSASSINATED

President William McKinley was shot and killed as he shook hands with well-wishers in Buffalo, New York. His assassin was a 28-year-old anarchist named Leon Czolgosz. An anarchist is someone who doesn't believe in any sort of rules or government.

McKinley's last words expressed concern for his wife, who had been ill since the deaths of their two baby daughters.

Vice-president Theodore Roosevelt was then sworn in as president. At 42 years old, Roosevelt was the youngest man ever to hold the office.

THE UMPIRE STRIKES BACK

Baseball's National League expelled Joe "Iron Man" Mc-Ginnity in August 1901. Witnesses claimed that he stepped on an umpire's toes, punched him, and spit in his face.

But, as it turned out, McGinnity was too popular a player to be expelled. Fans pleaded and begged, and finally the League gave in. After paying a stiff fine and apologizing, McGinnity was allowed to play again.

GETTING RID OF THE DUST—THE VACUUM CLEANER

The first attempt at a "dust-removing machine" wasn't very efficient. It was a big metal box with a chamber of compressed air. The machine sent shots of air into a carpet. The dust was forced out, and was collected in the box.

An Englishman named H. Cecil Booth thought the idea needed improving, since most of the dirt and dust missed the box and ended up back on the rug. He thought, why not suck the dust in, rather than blow it out?

Booth tried out the idea on a chair in a fancy restaurant, sucking with his mouth. Sure enough, clouds of dust came flying into his throat. Not a pleasant experience, thought Booth, but a worthwhile one.

He experimented with various kinds of filters. He wanted to find one that would trap the dust but allow the air from a pump to circulate. In 1901 he finally succeeded. The vacuum cleaner was born. The first model was heavy and large—about the size of a modern refrigerator.

The invention was valuable to people's health because it removed pounds of germs and dust from chairs and carpets in theaters, restaurants, and other public buildings. Booth's first job with his new vacuum cleaner was to clean the rug in Westminster Abbey for the coronation of Edward VII.

NEW RAZOR INTRODUCED

American businessman King Camp Gillette called his new razor the Safety Razor. The razor's sharp blades were enclosed in a holder shaped like a tiny garden hoe. The thin blades were to be used until they got dull, and then thrown away. Gillette's best friend, who had invented the throwaway bottlecap, had urged Gillette to invent something disposable. Gillette's Safety Razor was a big success.

12

EXPLOSIVE NOBEL PRIZES

The Alfred Nobel Prizes were first awarded in 1901. The Nobel Prizes were given to a few special people who had worked for the betterment of the human race.

Among those winning the prize this first year were Wilhelm Roentgen from Germany and Jean-Henri Dunant of Switzerland. Roentgen discovered the X ray, and Dunant founded the Red Cross.

Alfred Nobel, whose estate pays for these prizes, invented dynamite. He became one of the richest men in the world. To ease his mind about the terrible destruction his invention could cause, he established the awards that bear his name.

FANNIE FARMER'S COOKING SCHOOL

Fannie Farmer opened her famous cooking school in 1902. She vowed to change cooking into a more scientific process. She pledged to do away with such hard-to-understand terms as "a pinch" and "a dash." She adopted more standard measurements.

Fannie Farmer had suffered a stroke while still in high school and turned all her energies to cooking. She had been the cook at her family's boardinghouse and had won honors at the Boston Cooking School.

She did, indeed, change the way Americans cooked. She was known as the "Mother of the Level Measurement." Fannie Farmer was responsible for the wide use of oven thermometers and measuring cups!

COOLER SUMMERS AHEAD!

A year after he graduated from college, a young engineer named Willis Carrier invented the air conditioner. A printer had hired him to solve the problem of constantly changing temperatures in his print shop. Such changes affect the quality of printing. The printer needed help.

By adapting a steam heater to use cold water, and then by circulating the cool air with a fan, Carrier found that he also removed humidity from the air. This made the air even cooler!

A TRAGEDY AT ST. PIERRE

Everyone thought the volcano of Mt. Pelée was inactive. The volcano is on the island of Martinique, in the West Indies. But it exploded on May 8.

A few days before the final explosion, the volcano spewed ash and poisonous gases. Witnesses say hundreds of birds breathed the gases. Soon afterwards, they fell dead in the streets of St. Pierre.

14

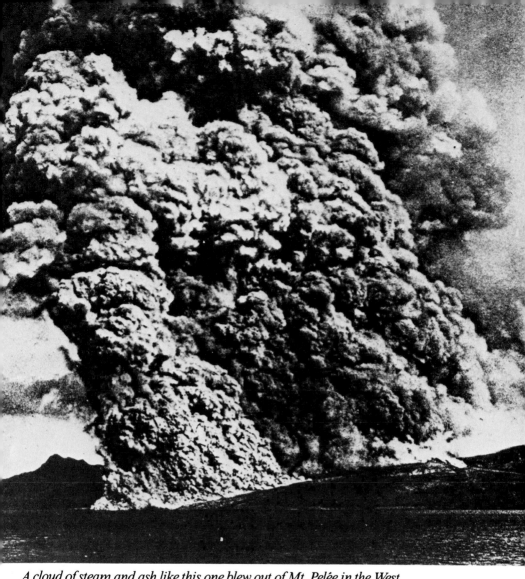

A cloud of steam and ash like this one blew out of Mt. Pelée in the West Indies when the volocano erupted violently in 1902.

When Mt. Pelée finally erupted, it did so with speed and force. A cloud of steam, poison gas, and smoke poured out of the top. It covered the town of St. Pierre. Within three minutes, more than 30,000 people were dead.

A coal mining camp

MINERS ON STRIKE

More than 145,000 coal miners in Pennsylvania walked off the job in 1902. They were angry at their low pay and dangerous working conditions. Poisonous gases and explosions were constant threats. Miners feared the deadly "black lung disease," caused by inhaling coal dust. For such hazardous work, miners were paid about $2 per day.

Because not all were sympathetic to the miners' cause, progress in the strike was very slow. One foe of the miners' complaints was their boss, George Baer, president of one of the largest coal companies. He was quoted as heartlessly saying that miners "don't suffer—they don't even speak English."

16

NO MORE SOLDIER BLUES

The United States Army decided in 1902 to change the color of soldiers' uniforms. The new ones would be a drab olive green. The previous color was blue, which proved too good a target in the Spanish-American war.

BLIBBER BLUBBER?

In 1902, Frank Fleer developed an early form of bubble gum. He called it Blibber Blubber. However, the gum was too sticky and didn't hold together well. In 1928, he reintroduced a new, improved version of the gum with a different name—Dubble Bubble.

SPELLING SHORTCUTS

The National Education Association decided that shortened spellings would be allowed for a few words. Among the approved new spellings were *program* for *programme, thru* for *through,* and *catalog* for *catalogue.*

JAZZ CATCHING ON

For many years, jazz music was considered more black than white. The reason is simple—jazz had its beginnings in several different kinds of music, especially African tribal music. The rhythms had been passed down through generations.

But in 1902, jazz broke out of the black community and became popular with whites, too. One of the reasons was the genius of Scott Joplin, a black jazz musician. The thirty-three-year-old Joplin captured the public's attention when he wrote "The Maple Leaf Rag."

Joplin's appeal was not limited to his own time. His song "The Entertainer" was used as the theme song for the 1973 movie *The Sting.*

1902

17

FROM COAST TO COAST

August 21 was the last day of a grueling coast-to-coast automobile trip. Splattered with mud, the car pulled into New York City, still in excellent shape. The Model F Packard was driven by Tom Fetch of the Packard Company and a writer named M. C. Karrup.

The two drivers tried to average about 80 miles each day. Starting their journey in San Francisco, they drove along the shore so that the car's tires would actually touch the Pacific Ocean. They tried to end the same way, by having the tires touch the Atlantic, but bad weather caused them to change their plan.

TAKE ME OUT TO THE BALL GAME

The first-ever World Series was played in October 1903. Baseball had only one league, the National, for many years. It didn't have any competition until 1901, when the American League was added.

Boston of the new American League upset Pittsburgh, of the National League, five games to three. Cy Young, the ace pitcher for Boston, won two of the five games.

PANAMA NO LONGER PART OF SOUTH AMERICA!

In November, the United States formally recognized the new nation of Panama. Once part of the South American nation of Colombia, Panama was the site of a planned canal linking the Atlantic and Pacific oceans. When the canal was completed, the little nation would be a part of North America.

When Colombia earlier had rejected a $10 million offer from the United States, some groups in the country revolted. Fearing that they would lose money if the canal were not built, they declared themselves an independent country called Panama. The United States supported the revolt and quickly recognized the new country. Some historians claim that Americans planned

18

The new nation of Panama eventually became the site of the Panama Canal.

the revolt so they could build and control the canal.

The canal would have many advantages. For one thing, ships traveling from New York to California would no longer have to sail all the way around South America. By cutting through the proposed canal, almost 7,900 extra miles would be saved!

"IT'S THE REAL THING"

In 1903, the popular soft drink Coca-Cola changed its list of ingredients. The cocaine that had been a part of the formula since Coke's invention in 1886 was removed. The drug caffeine was substituted.

The rest of the formula for Coca-Cola is still a secret. In fact, only the top two executives of the company know what it is. That's why they are prohibited, by company rules, from ever traveling together. If an accident should happen and both of the executives were killed, the formula would be lost forever.

Teddy bears, which were named after President Theodore Roosevelt, became the rage in 1903.

THE ROOSEVELT BEAR

One of the most popular toys of all time—the teddy bear— was first marketed in 1903. Did you know that the teddy was named after President Theodore Roosevelt?

When President Roosevelt visited Mississippi, he had a little time to do some hunting. But he didn't have much luck all day. His southern hosts felt embarrassed by the lack of game. They trapped a young bear for him to shoot. President Roosevelt shook his head. No, he couldn't shoot a cub, especially one that was being released just so he could gun it down.

The story of the president's kindheartedness hit all the major newspapers. One store owner in Brooklyn, New York, made

After their historic first flight in 1903, Orville and Wilbur Wright flew their plane in many other successful flights at Kitty Hawk, North Carolina, such as this one in 1911.

a small stuffed bear. He put it in his window with a sign, "Teddy's Bear."

Customers went wild! Everyone wanted a little bear just like it. The store owner sold quite a few, and went on to form his own toy company. Other toymakers began making them, too. They couldn't keep up with the thousands of orders. Some called them "Roosevelt Bears," but most preferred just "Teddy."

AIRBORNE!

Wilbur and Orville Wright proved to the world that humans were not earthbound. It happened in Kitty Hawk, North Carolina on December 17. In four separate flights the two brothers got their airplane, *Flyer I,* off the ground.

Using a little 25-horsepower engine, the airplane's longest flight was about one minute. The Wright brothers were confident that this was only the beginning.

Their success contradicted the "proof" of a noted American scientist who, in the earlier part of 1903, had shown that air flight was impossible.

THE FIREMAN WHO DIDN'T WANT TO BE BALD

In 1904, a young fireman from Massachusetts named John Breck was concerned. His hair was falling out, and he was soon going to be bald. He didn't like the idea one bit.

In his free time, he experimented with different medications to put on his scalp. His experiments became more and more time-consuming, however, so he gave up his fireman's job to devote as much time as he could to finding the cure for baldness.

Over the years he came up with many hair care products. Today his formulas for shampoo are still popular. Yet Breck, as successful as he was at developing these rinses, shampoos, and scalp conditioners, never found the cure he was looking for!

GUNPOWDER AND A GUILTY CONSCIENCE

A secret code from the thirteenth century was finally cracked in 1904 but, as it turned out, nobody really cared.

Roger Bacon had invented gunpowder in the 1200s. But instead of advertising his discovery, and perhaps earning some hard cash, he panicked. Fearing that people might use his invention to hurt one another, he wrote the formula down in a complicated code.

Of course, his invention was duplicated by others. That is often the case when people invent things. Many discoveries are made by more than one person. After his death, different people in many different parts of the world figured out how to make gunpowder, too. By the time a cryptographer, or code-cracker, deciphered Bacon's code, the damage Bacon had feared had already taken place. And it wasn't even his fault!

THE FIRST PERFECT GAME

Boston pitcher Cy Young pitched major league baseball's first perfect game on May 5. A perfect game is different from a no-hitter in that in a perfect game the pitcher allows no batter to reach first base, not even on a walk!

The memorable Cy Young in action

A TRAGIC FIRE AND A BAD MISTAKE

On June 15, over 1,000 people died in a fire on board a steamboat in New York City. The ship, named the *General Slocum*, was on the East River. Fire suddenly roared through the boat. Most of the passengers were mothers and their children on their way to a church picnic. Few could swim.

The captain of the boat made an error that may have cost many lives. Instead of heading toward the shore 300 feet away, he turned and headed out toward North Brother Island, much farther away.

As shocked people looked on from the shore, hundreds of women and children were burned. Many of the women, knowing they were about to be consumed by the flames, threw their babies into the water. They hoped that some miracle would save them.

JUDO IN THE OVAL OFFICE?

In 1904, the ancient Oriental martial art of judo was becoming more popular in the United States. Part of that surge in popularity came after President Theodore Roosevelt publicly announced that he was taking lessons. A judo master was going to the White House once a week!

A TASTY INVENTION

St. Louis, Missouri, was the site of the 1904 World's Fair. Thousands of people from all over the world came to admire the achievements of each country. Particularly popular were the many food booths and displays. It was at one of these booths that the ice cream cone was invented.

The Palace of Liberal Arts was one of the fancy buildings constructed for the 1904 World's Fair in St. Louis.

Ice cream was already a popular dessert, eaten in a dish or sometimes on waffles. A young man who was working in a booth selling ice cream ran out of paper dishes. Suddenly he hit upon an idea. Taking a waffle from the vendor next door, he rolled it into a cone shape and stuck a scoop of ice cream on the top.

You can guess the rest—thousands of people wanted to sample the new creation. It wasn't called an "ice cream cone" at first, however. The official name was "World's Fair Cornucopia."

25

Football players in the early 1900s wore little or no padding. Jim Thorpe, the great Native American athlete, played with little protection.

MAKE IT SAFER!

Football had become so violent by 1905 that a special panel was established to make it safer. So rough was it, in fact, that after seeing a picture of a bruised and battered college player, President Theodore Roosevelt declared that the game should be outlawed.

Of course it wasn't outlawed, but it was made safer. One change was that forward passes became legal. Also, the amount of yards needed to be gained was increased to ten.

The panel also called for stricter officiating. They urged that referees be selected by one governing body to ensure more consistent calling of fouls and penalties.

WHO'S GOT THE BALL?

Speaking of football, a trick play was becoming popular in 1905. In the "hidden ball maneuver," one player stuffed the ball in the back of his teammate's jersey. The player would then amble innocently toward the goal line. It sounds crazy, but it often worked.

The play was first introduced in 1903 by famous college coach "Pop" Warner. He remembered that some of his players had been fooling around with the stunt in practice. So, he thought, why not try it? There was no word from the new rules committee on whether the hidden ball maneuver would be outlawed.

A DANGEROUS INGREDIENT

Although a medicine called Mrs. Winslow's Soothing Syrup was labeled in England as poisonous early in 1905, it continued to be sold in the United States. It was marketed as a remedy to ease the pain of teething babies. Unfortunately, the relief to countless babies was provided by a secret ingredient—the highly addictive drug morphine.

MAKEUP GAINING RESPECTABILITY

Rouge was advertised in the Sears catalog for the first time in 1905. Called by its French name, *rouge de théâtre* was still thought of as something only for actresses or bar dancers. Most American women wore no makeup at all, but times were changing. In the next few years, the French makeup industry—with such names as Chanel and Dior—would take America by storm.

THE LARGEST DIAMOND ON EARTH

A diamond company in South Africa announced in January that it had found the largest diamond ever. It was reported to be as big as a man's fist.

The diamond was discovered by one of the supervisors of the mine. When he first saw it, he thought it was glass—surely no diamond that big existed.

Experts confirmed soon afterward that indeed it was a diamond—all 1.3 pounds of it—and a very precious one, at that. It was immediately insured. It was also given a name—the Cullinan diamond, after the man who had opened the mine three years earlier.

PROGRESS FOR WOMEN SLOW

A law allowing women to vote received another setback from former President Grover Cleveland. In an interview published in the *Ladies' Home Journal,* Cleveland stated that suffrage, or voting, by women was wrong, and that supporters were misled. "No sensible and responsible woman wants to vote," declared the former President.

"THE FASTEST LONG-DISTANCE TRAINS ON EARTH"

The United States proudly announced the two fastest long-distance trains in the world. They were the Pennsylvania Rail-

May Sutton

road's train that went from New York to Chicago in only 18 hours, and the New York Central's line that went the same distance in about the same time.

"The fastest" didn't mean "the safest," however. Within one week of the announcement, both trains had bad accidents, leaving 19 people dead.

AN UPROAR AT WIMBLEDON

Famous women's singles tennis player May Sutton caused an uproar at the Wimbledon Championship Tournament in June. She dared to come out on the court dressed in a white tennis dress which rose almost two inches above her ankles!

May, a 17-year-old American, was given an order by the tennis officials. She had to lower the hem on her dress, or she wouldn't be allowed to play. She did and play continued. The results? May won in two sets — 6–3, 6–4.

1906

47 TERRIFYING SECONDS

San Francisco, California, suffered the worst earthquake in the history of the United States on April 18. Lasting only 47 seconds, it killed more than 700 people and caused millions of dollars worth of damage. Over 250 miles of land literally shifted 21 feet to the north. In the process, buildings, roads, and homes wobbled and folded. Thousands were trapped, waiting until someone heard their cries for help.

Fires broke out around the city, too, and many people were injured by falling debris. Police and volunteer rescue workers searched round the clock for survivors. Many were trapped or hurt in the earthquake. Others were in a panic trying to get out of the city. Certain that another earthquake would follow, thousands of San Franciscans lined up at the docks. They tried to buy tickets for ships leaving the city.

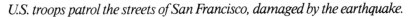

U.S. troops patrol the streets of San Francisco, damaged by the earthquake.

View of San Francisco after the devastating earthquake and the fires that followed

HOT DOGS

In 1906, Americans were still calling those sausages on long buns many different things—frankfurters, wieners, and even dachshund sausages, after the very long dog with the very short legs.

That summer a newspaper cartoonist sketched one of the little dogs in a bun with mustard all over it. Below the cartoon, the artist wanted to print, "Get your red-hot dachshund sausages!" There was a little problem, however. The cartoonist didn't know how to spell "dachshund."

A quick flick of the pencil here, a little erasing there, and the cartoon was then captioned, "Get your hot dogs." The name stuck.

31

A SPACE SAVER

A young inventor from Paris, France, invented the first collapsible baby stroller in 1906. E. Baumann, like many Parisians, lived in an apartment. He knew that anything that could save a little space was worth its weight in gold.

DISEASE-CARRIER FOUND AT LAST

For eight years, public health workers had been looking for someone. They knew this person was a carrier of the deadly disease typhoid. In 1906 she was found. Nicknamed "Typhoid Mary," the woman had worked as a cook in several homes and institutions. Everywhere she worked people would come down with the disease. But she would leave before anyone figured out that she was to blame.

Mary was a carrier of the disease. However, she was not sick with it herself—only very contagious to others. She was ordered to be isolated until her death. She died in 1938. There was no known cure for the disease, nor any way of changing her status as a carrier.

After a search of eight years, "Typhoid Mary" was found and isolated so she could not spread the disease any further.

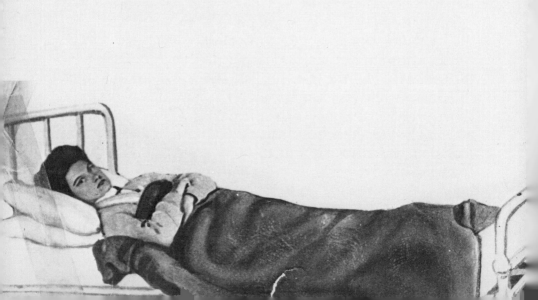

NEW "WAVE"

A London hairdresser found a new way to create exciting hairstyles—especially for those with straight hair. Charles Nestle found that by dipping a lock of hair in ammonia, wrapping it around a safety pin and heating it with an iron, the hair would take on a "permanent" wave. The curl lasted several months. English women were a little cautious about the whole thing. American women, however, were very enthusiastic. The "permanent," as it became known, turned out to be quite the fashion. Although Nestle's idea has been changed a little, the concept is the same today.

SOME FRIGHTENING FACTS

Upton Sinclair published a book that forever changed the way Americans thought about food. *The Jungle* was about day-to-day activities in a meat packing house. The book described in stomach-churning detail the ingredients that ended up in meat—rats crushed in grinders, bugs of all varieties, animal waste, all kinds of dirt swept off the floor, and even pieces of fingers cut off by sharp knives. The book also had many examples of sick animals being butchered, and sick workers packing up the meat.

Sinclair intended to make people aware of the filth in many of the places that produced America's food. He hoped that by making people angry, they would demand reforms. They did.

As a result of Sinclair's book, President Roosevelt signed the Pure Food and Drug Act into law on June 30. The new law required government inspections of meat before it could leave the packing houses. Also, the law made it a crime for companies to mislabel food products or medicines. It was hoped that these changes would make food production safer and healthier.

WEIGHING THE SOUL

Many religions teach that when a person dies, his or her soul leaves the body. Could this really be true? In 1907, Massachusetts doctor Duncan MacDougall decided to find out.

Dr. MacDougall made a large scale and put on it the bed of a dying man. Carefully weighing the man in his bed, Dr. Mac-Dougall kept precise measurements. He did this every hour until the man died. Immediately after the man died, MacDougall weighed him again. According to his findings, the dead man weighed about an ounce less than he had moments before he died!

Dr. MacDougall tried the experiment on other patients. The results were the same. The difference between the living person and the dead seemed to be anywhere between half an ounce and one ounce.

Newspapers in 1907 published the story, and many scoffed at MacDougall, calling him a religious fanatic.

"EVERYBODY WANTS TO BE FRANK!"

In the early 1900s, kids were reading about a boy detective named Frank Merriwell. He was a star athlete and all-around great kid. Gilbert Patten, the author of the popular books, said kids liked to imagine that they, too, tracked criminals and won exciting races. "Everybody wants to be Frank," said Patten. "He's part of every kid growing up."

Frank appeared in *Tip Top Weekly,* a magazine that cost a nickel. For 15 cents, kids could buy a hardbound book with longer stories.

DOUBLE PLAY!

Baseball's double play was fast becoming routine for one team. The Chicago Cubs had three players who could turn al-

A cover of the popular Tip Top Weekly *magazine*

M. BROWN.   J.PFEISTER   A.HOFMAN   C.G.WILLIAMS   O.OVERALL.   E.REULBACH.   J.KLING.
H.GESSLER.   J.TAYLOR.   H.STEINFELDT.   J.McCORMICK.   F.CHANCE.   J.SHECKARD.   P.MORAN.   F. SCHULTE.
C.LUNDGREN.   T.WALSH.   J. EVERS.   J. SLAGLE.   J.TINKER.

CHICAGO NATIONAL LEAGUE BALL CLUB 1906

Tinker, Evers, and Chance were stars of both the 1906 and 1907 Chicago Cubs.

most any ground ball hit in the infield into a surefire double play. The players were Joe Tinker, Johnny Evers, and Frank Chance. So precise were they, in fact, that these three names from 1907 have become another way of saying "easy as pie"—Tinker, to Evers, to Chance!

MOTHER'S DAY

A young woman from West Virginia named Anna Jarvis felt sad—her mother had died, and Jarvis was nagged by feelings of guilt. She felt that perhaps she hadn't done enough for her mother. She also felt maybe she hadn't told her mother how much she loved her.

In 1907, she had an idea. On the second Sunday in May (which was the anniversary of her mother's death) she invited some friends over to her house. Jarvis proposed that they try to make a national holiday honoring all mothers. This way others would remember to tell their own mothers how much they were loved.

36

The guests agreed, and they set to work writing letters and trying to get support. For a holiday to be made an official national holiday, Congress and the president had to sign it into law.

Jarvis and her supporters began locally in their hometown in West Virginia. The following year, on the second Sunday in May, the Sunday sermon centered on the importance of mothers throughout history. At the end of the service, Jarvis handed out flowers to all the mothers.

Mother's Day continued to gain in popularity, as more and more towns adopted the idea. Finally a massive letter-writing campaign was begun. People wrote to their congressmen and urged them to vote the holiday into law. As one senator remarked, "It became positively un-American not to support Mother's Day!"

In 1914, Anna Jarvis's idea became law. Seven years from its beginning, the holiday honoring mothers everywhere was official.

THE 46TH STATE

On November 16, Oklahoma officially became the 46th state in the union. Naming the new state, however, provoked much controversy.

Many whites and Native Americans had hoped the state would be named Sequoyah, after the famous Cherokee Indian. Many historians thought Sequoyah was the most influential of all Native Americans. He had done many things to improve the Cherokee way of life, and had developed a written alphabet for the Cherokee language.

But Congress refused to adopt the name. Instead, the state was named with a combination of two Choctaw Native American words. Deeply disappointed, many members of the Cherokee tribe of the time viewed the decision as an insult.

CLEANER COFFEE

A German woman named Melitta Bentz was dissatisfied with the coffee she served her family. She thought it would taste much better if some of the grit and impurities were filtered out.

Using a two-chambered coffeepot, she tried different fabrics to see which would trap the most grit. Cotton worked for a short while, but it soon shredded. Finally she tried cutting out a section of her ink blotter. Blotter paper was strong and porous. It worked wonderfully.

The filter system for coffee that Melitta invented is still popular today. The company that sells the filters still bears her name.

FOR ONLY A NICKEL

Nickelodeons, or little movie houses, became quite the rage in 1908. About 8,000 of them cropped up across the country, showing movies continuously. Since sound hadn't been invented yet, a piano player would provide a musical accompaniment to the action on the screen.

The nickelodeon was appropriately named, for the experience cost a customer only a nickel.

Ford's Model T was called the "car that put America on wheels."

ON WHEELS

Henry Ford introduced his new Model T in August. Nick-named "the Tin Lizzie," it was touted as "easy to drive" by the average person. Earlier cars had almost made it necessary for the driver to be a mechanic, since the engines were always needing repairs.

The Model T was also quicker to make. Assembly line workers could put one together in just over 14 hours. The price of a 1908 Model T was $850. Ford would sell 15 million of the cars— "in any color, as long as it's black!"

Local residents stand outside a popular nickelodeon movie house.

1908

FIRST AIR CRASH FATALITY

On September 17, a 26-year-old army lieutenant became the first person in history to die in an airplane crash. The victim, Thomas E. Selfridge, rode in a plane piloted by inventor Orville Wright. Wright was injured, but not severely.

The crash took place before a crowd of 2,000 spectators in Fort Myer, Virginia. Wright had experimented with the plane to meet the needs of the army. For one thing, the army required that the plane be able to travel at least 40 miles per hour.

The crash occurred because of a broken propeller blade on the left side of the aircraft. Even though this was a tragedy, the army was eager to continue experimenting with the airplane. Aviation added a whole new dimension to our national defense.

Orville Wright and a French count talk after a successful flight in Paris in 1908. But not all of the Wright brothers' flights were successful.

USE IT AND THROW IT AWAY!

The paper cup was invented in 1908, although its inventor was actually trying to accomplish something else. A New Englander named Hugh Moore had come up with the idea of public water machines—large vats with containers for ice, water, and paper cups. The paper cups were waxy on the inside and could be discarded after each use. Moore charged one penny for a drink from these machines.

However, the idea didn't really catch on. People preferred their old public fountains, which involved holding a tin dipper under a pump. Everyone, sick and healthy alike, used the dipper. No one really thought about the transfer of disease—and certainly no one wanted to pay for a cup of water!

A public health officer came to Moore's rescue. Dr. Samuel Crumbine wrote articles about the horrible diseases and germs one could catch by using the public dipper. Several states decided to ban their use, and Moore's paper cups were a great and healthy substitute. At first he named his company Health Kups, but later changed it to the more interesting-sounding Dixie Cups.

KEWPIES

Another popular item in 1908 was the Kewpie doll. The Kewpie got its name from Cupid, the chubby little angel seen on valentines. Kewpies were first popular as drawings. But soon there were Kewpie dolls—anywhere from 2 to 14 inches tall. In a matter of months the Kewpies had gotten so popular that they were added as decorations on just about everything. There were Kewpie perfume, Kewpie wastebaskets, Kewpie dishtowels, and Kewpie inkwells.

They weren't just for children, either. Store clerks claimed that most of the Kewpies were sold to women who wanted them just for themselves!

A NEW PRESIDENT

On March 4, William Howard Taft was inaugurated as the 27th president of the United States. The inauguration took place in the middle of a blizzard that gripped Washington, DC.

Since Taft had been secretary of war under Theodore Roosevelt, Roosevelt chose Taft as his successor. This recommendation helped him in the election. Taft beat William Jennings Bryan, whom Roosevelt had beaten once as well.

Taft was the fattest president ever. Weighing about 330 pounds, he once became stuck in the White House bathtub during his first year as president. Aides and bodyguards had to remove him.

THE BEGINNINGS OF HAIR DYE

Throughout the years, there have been different methods by which women would try changing the color of their hair. Often the methods were unsafe or even painful—rashes, skin sores, and allergic reactions were common.

In 1909, a French chemist named Eugene Schueller developed the first commercial hair dye—packaged to be sold in stores. He used a newer (and milder) chemical that made the process much safer than it had been before.

Schueller named his product Harmless Hair Dye. It sold well, or at least as well as any hair dye could in those days. After all, in the early 1900s only about three percent of women dyed their hair. Today Schueller's company is still in business, although he decided to change the name—to L'Oréal. And the number of women who color their hair has increased to 75 percent!

William Howard Taft, the 27th president of the United States

THE TOP OF THE WORLD

On April 6, Commander Robert Peary of the United States Navy and Matthew Henson were the first people to reach the North Pole. Along with four Inuit assistants and 40 sled dogs, they reached their frozen destination. It had taken 36 days of grueling travel over the worst conditions imaginable.

Upon reaching the Pole, Peary planted an American flag. But when he returned to the United States, his moment of glory was spoiled because another man claimed to have reached the North Pole in 1908.

Dr. Frederick Cook, a one-time associate of Peary, argued that he had been there before Peary. He claimed he had buried a tube containing an American flag in the snow. The matter was left up to a committee from the University of Copenhagen in Denmark.

After reviewing much evidence, and after interviewing several of the Eskimos who accompanied Cook, the committee made their unanimous decision. Peary had reached the Pole first. According to Cook's traveling companions, their expedition had stopped miles short of the North Pole.

Cook was accused of being "shameless" and an impostor, while Peary received admiration and a gold medal from the National Geographic Society.

Commander Robert Peary

INDEX

Film star Mary Pickford at the start of her career